A GIFT FOR

_____

For this child I prayed.
1 SAMUEL 1:27 AMP

FROM

_____

BE SAFE LITTLE
Boy

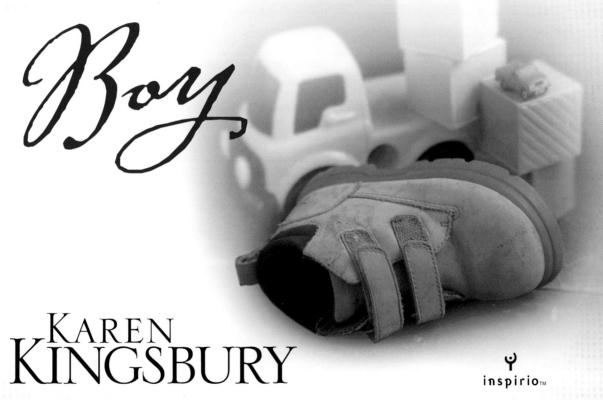

WORDS OF LOVE FOR MOMS

BE SAFE LITTLE

Boy

KAREN KINGSBURY

inspirio™

Dedicated to . . .

Donald, my prince charming,
Kelsey, my precious daughter,
Tyler, my beautiful song,
Sean, my wonder boy,
Josh, my tender tough guy,
EJ, my chosen one,
Austin, my miracle child,

And to God Almighty, the author of life,
who has—for now—blessed me with these.

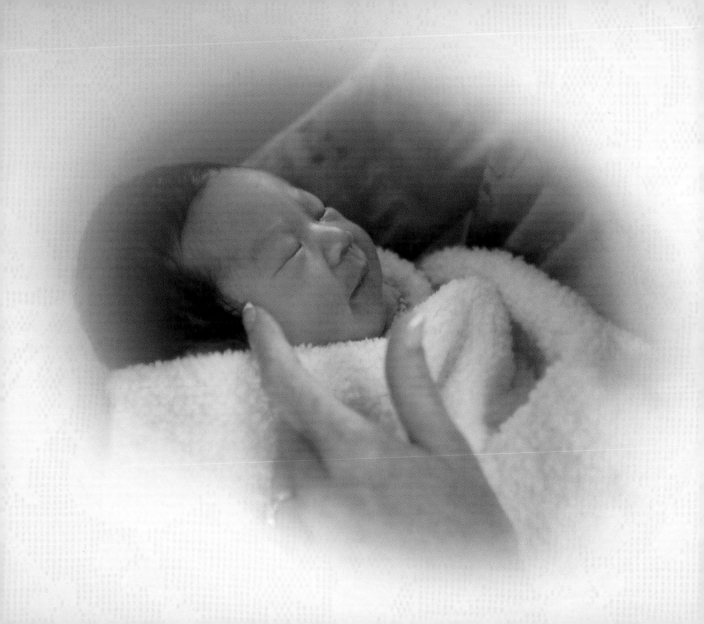

*O*ne day a little boy was
born into the world
and for a very small moment,
his mother held him close.

$\mathcal{B}$ut soon they came to clean him up
and right then the mother knew.
Life with that little boy
would always mean letting him go.

Time passed and the little boy became a one-year-old.
His mother knew something had changed because
the little boy didn't want to be held anymore—
he wanted to walk. So she kissed him on top of his head,
took a seat at the back of the room, and held her breath
and crookedly, very crookedly, he took his first steps.
From the place where she watched him,
that mother hummed a quiet hum.
And in her heart the words went something like this:

Be safe little boy,

Don't you fall little boy,

Look how fast you've grown.

Be safe little boy, where you walk little boy

You're not yet on your own.

The boy grew older and for his sixth birthday
he got a shiny bike. His mother knew it was time
to let go a little more. So she kissed him on the top of his helmet,
stood back, and slowly, very slowly, he climbed onto the seat.
From the place where she watched him start to ride,
that mother whistled a quiet whistle. And in her heart,
the words went something like this:

Be safe little boy,

Pedal hard little boy,

Look how much you've grown.

Be safe little boy, where you ride little boy,

You're not yet on your own.

*Y*ears passed and the boy became a fourth grader.
His mother knew it was time for him to walk to school
each morning by himself. So on the first day,
she kissed him goodbye, stood back, and quickly, very quickly,
he ran to meet his friends. From the place where she watched him
start out, that mother sang a quiet song. And in her heart,
the words went something like this:

Be safe little boy,

Watch for cars little boy,

Look how much you've grown.

Be safe little boy, where you go little boy,

You'll soon be on your own.

Middle school came and the boy became a football player. Football was rough and tough and sometimes boys got hurt, but his mother knew it was time to let him play. So she helped him with his shoulder pads, kissed him for good luck, stayed at the top of the bleachers, and wildly, very wildly, he tackled and ran and won that game. From the place where she watched him play, that mother thought a quiet thought. And in her heart, the words went something like this:

Be safe little boy,

Don't get hurt little boy,

Look how much you've grown.

Be safe little boy, where you play little boy,

You're almost on your own.

*M*ore time passed and the boy learned to drive.
Driving was scary for his mother, because sometimes
she wouldn't know where he was or if he was okay.
But his mother knew it was time to give him the keys.
So she found him a car, kissed him on the cheek,
stayed at the top of the driveway, and carefully,
very carefully, he backed down the hill and drove out of sight.
From the place where she watched him leave,
that mother prayed a quiet prayer. And in her heart,
the words went something like this:

Be safe little boy,

Buckle up little boy,

Look how much you've grown.

Be safe little boy, where you drive little boy,

You're almost on your own.

The years went by crazy fast and the boy fell in love.
Love meant that his mother would have to share
her little boy's heart with someone else, but she knew it was time
for him to take that journey. So she helped him order flowers,
blew him a kiss as he drove off, and gladly, very gladly he went to find his girl.
From the place where she watched him leave, that mother whispered
a quiet whisper. And in her heart, the words went something like this:

Be safe little boy,

Guard your heart little boy,

Look how much you've grown.

Be safe little boy, where you love little boy,

It's time you're on your own.

*T*wo more years passed and the boy was getting married and moving away.
Marriage meant his mother might not see her boy much.
Maybe not at all. But she knew her boy loved the girl, and it was time
to plan a wedding. So she helped him find a fancy suit, kissed them both
as they finished their vows, and suddenly, very suddenly,
her little boy was gone. From the place where she watched them
walk out of the church, that mother cried a little cry.
And in her heart, the words went something like this:

Be safe little boy,

Don't forget me, little boy,

Look how much you've grown.

Be safe little boy, where you leave little boy,

You're finally on your own.

A lifetime went by in the blink of an eye,
and the mother grew old. So old, she had only a
little while before God called her home to heaven.
But she knew where she was going—and she told her boy
so—when she called him to her side and said goodbye.
This time the boy leaned over and kissed her on the cheek, and barely,
very barely, she squeezed his hand. From the place where she lay,
she looked at her son's eyes and breathed a last little breath.
And in her heart, the words went something like this:

Be safe little boy,

Cling to God little boy,

And one day you'll come home.

Be safe little boy, where you go little boy,

You'll never be alone.

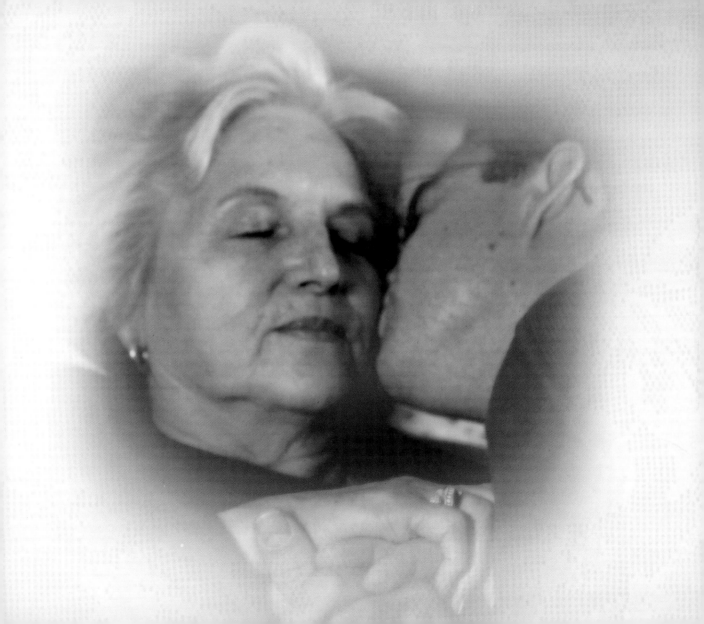

Stay Close Little Girl:
Words of Love for Dads

Format: Hardcover, Jacketed

Page Count: 48

List Price: $9.99 {CDN:$13.99}

Size: 7-3/4 x 6-1/2

ISBN: 0-310-81447-2

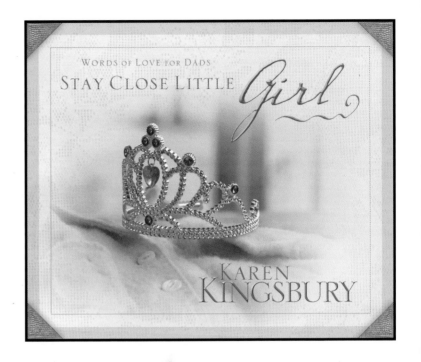

Especially for dads, this heartwarming poem from best-selling author Karen Kingsbury talks about the importance of keeping your little girl close as she grows up so fast! Includes original photography featuring racially diverse dads and daughters.

Even Now

Format: Softcover

Page Count: 368

List Price: $14.99 {CDN:$20.99}

Size: 5-1/2 x 8-1/2

ISBN: 0-310-24753-5

A young woman seeking answers to her heart's deep questions. A man and woman separated by lies and long years, who have never forgotten each other. With hallmark tenderness and power, Karen Kingsbury weaves a tapestry of lives, losses, love, and faith—and the miracle of resurrection.

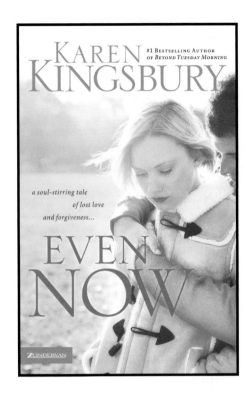

At Inspirio, we love to hear from you—
your stories, your feedback,
and your product ideas.
Please send your comments to us
by way of email at
icares@zondervan.com
or to the address below:

inspirio

Attn: Inspirio Cares
5300 Patterson Avenue SE
Grand Rapids, MI 49530

If you would like further information
about Inspirio and the products we
create, please visit us at:
www.inspiriogifts.com

Thank you and God bless!